Alexander Graham Bell

Father of Modern Communication

Michael Pollard

BLACKBIRCH PRESS, INC.

WOODBRIDGE, CONNECTICUT

Published by Blackbirch Press, Inc.
260 Amity Road
Woodbridge, CT 06525
web site: http://www.blackbirch.com
e-mail: staff@blackbirch.com

First published in Great Britain as *Scientists Who Have Changed the World* by Exley Publications Ltd., Chalk Hill, Watford, 1990.
© Exley Publications, Ltd., 1990
© Michael Pollard, 1990

10 9 8 7 6 5 4 3 2 1

Photo Credits:
AT&T: Cover, 6, 34, 51; Bell Canada Historical Source: 30; The Bostonian Society/The Old State House: 16-7; The Bridgeman Art Library: 12, 13: British Telecommunications: 53, 55 all, 58, 59 below; Mary Evans Picture Library: 8 and 9 (Bruce Castle Museum), 10, 51; Exley Publications: 29 (Nick Birch), 32; Michael Holford: 46; New York Historical Society: 50; Telecom Technology Showcase (British Telecom Museum): 44 (top), 47; Telefocus (British Telecom): 4; Library of Congress: 7, 19, 21, 24, and 25 (Gilbert H. Grosvenor Collection), 26, 31 (top) and 35 (National Geographic Society), 31 (below) (Gilbert H. Grosvenor Collection), 36, 38-9, 40-1, 45, 49, and 56 (Gilbert H. Grosvenor Collection), 60 (National Geographic Society); Magnum: 59 (top) (Eric Hartmann); Royal National Institute for the Deaf: 14-5; Zefa: 54.

Printed in China

70

Library of Congress Cataloging-in-Publication Data
Pollard, Michael.
     Alexander Graham Bell : father of modern communication / by Michael Pollard —1st
     U.S. ed.
           p. cm.—(Giants of science)
     Includes index.
     Summary: Examines the life and accomplishments of the speech teacher whose study of sound and the human voice led to his invention of the telephone.
     ISBN 1-56711-334-6 (hardcover : alk. paper)
     1. Bell, Alexander Graham, 1847-1922—Juvenile literature. 2. Inventors—United States—Biography—Juvenile literature. [1. Bell, Alexander Graham, 1847-1922. 2. Inventors.] I. Title. II. Series.
TK6143.B4 P65 2000   00-008818
621.385'092—dc21   CIP
                                                           AC

Contents

Unsettled and Anxious

Among the passengers on the morning train from Boston to Washington on Saturday, February 26, 1876, was an anxious and impatient young man, age twenty-eight. Fashionably dressed in a long, dark cutaway coat, white shirt, and a black bow tie under a wing collar, he was visibly uncomfortable and unsettled. From time to time, he got up and paced the length of the coach. Frequently, he took his watch from his pocket and glanced at it. He tried to read his newspaper, but couldn't concentrate. Now and again, he took out a notebook and wrote a few words.

The young man, named Alexander Graham Bell, had good reason to be agitated. If things went well, he was on his way to making a fortune. If they went badly, he was on his way to nowhere.

Securing a Dream

A telegram had arrived the previous night at Bell's home in Boston. It was from his business partner Gardiner Greene Hubbard. The message asked Bell to leave for Washington as soon as possible.

Hubbard had gone to Washington two weeks earlier. There, he had filed details of an amazing new apparatus Bell had invented that could carry the sound of human speech through wires. This apparatus already had a name—the telephone—but as yet there was no working model. So far, Bell had managed to send only vague and indistinct noises over his telephone. But he was confident

Opposite:

Alexander Graham Bell is considered the Father of Modern Communication because of his many useful inventions.

5

This portrait of Alexander Graham Bell shows him in his attic laboratory in Boston.

that he was near success. All his life, Alexander Graham Bell had dreamed of making an earth-shaking invention. It seemed now that he was only days away from making that dream come true.

It was the protection of Bell's invention that made Gardiner Green Hubbard's trip to Washington so important. Hubbard's aim was to secure a patent for Bell's telephone. By giving full details of an invention and obtaining a patent, an inventor can prevent others from copying the idea and profiting from it. With a patent, the idea becomes the inventor's property. It can be sold to anyone else, or a fee can be demanded from anyone who wants to use it in business. In the United States at that time, a patent lasted for seventeen years. After that initial period, the patent "ran out" and was free for anyone to use.

Rivals

Much to his dismay, Bell had not been alone in his research. This was the reason for his hurried trip to Washington. He needed to be on hand in case officials at the United States Patent Office wanted to question him. Another inventor, Elisha Gray, had come up with an almost identical idea, and had applied for a patent on the very same day. It was up to the officials of the Patent Office to decide whether it would be Gray or Bell who went down in history as the inventor of the telephone.

Upon his arrival in Washington, Bell faced an anxious wait while Patent Office officials made their decision. "You can hardly understand the state of uncertainty and suspense in which I am now," Bell wrote to his father. The outcome of the patent applications was crucial. The winner would make a fortune from the right to make and sell telephones throughout the United States, and eventually all over the world.

A Powerful Rival

Soon after his arrival, Bell heard more worrying news. It seemed that a third application for a telephone patent had arrived. And it was in the name of someone who was already famous as an inventor: Thomas Alva Edison. Bell found out that Edison had the financial backing of America's leading telegraph company, the mighty Western Union.

Western Union was made up of many powerful men with influence in the most elite U.S. government circles in Washington. They had made huge profits from the telegraph business and had limitless money to spend. Bell had financial support from his partner, Hubbard, and another inventor, but it was nothing compared to the money Western Union could spend on supporting Edison. Bell's character was honest and open, and he hated

The operations room of the Western Union Telegraph Company. Founded in 1851, Western Union had a commanding position in the telegraph industry by 1875.

Until almost the middle of the nineteenth century, the fastest means of travel and communication was by horse. Here, a mail coach arrives at dawn at Temple Bar in the heart of London.

double-dealing. He was both angry and hurt when he suspected that some of the people he met in Washington while waiting for the patent applications were commercial spies from Western Union.

For the past nine months Bell had worked almost to the point of exhaustion, combining work on his invention with full-time university teaching. Now, he stood wondering: Was he going to be cheated out of the fame and fortune that was rightly his?

Decision Time

In the U. S. Patent Office, officials pored over the three patent applications for a so-called "telephone." Edison had not gone as far as the others in developing the idea of the "speaking telegraph" —as the telephone was called at first—though he had covered much of the same ground. Edison's application was soon eliminated, and the final choice lay between Elisha Gray and Alexander Graham Bell. Who had submitted the most accurate and practical description and drawings of a working telephone?

After five tense days, the Patent Office officials came to their decision. The patent would be awarded to Alexander Graham Bell.

Bell heard the news on his twenty-ninth birthday. It was certainly one of the most valuable and most welcome birthday presents that anyone had ever received!

Urgent government messages were often sent by express riders using relays of horses.

An Electric Revolution

Just as the twentieth century was sometimes called the computer age, the nineteenth century was above all the age of electricity. The work of British scientist Michael Faraday and others early in the century had revealed electricity to be a new source of energy for the world to exploit. One of the first ways it was utilized was in the field of communications.

It's hard to believe—but it is true—that until about 150 years ago, communications were still almost as slow and primitive as they had been in ancient Egypt 5,000 years before. In the 1840s, the newly built rail networks were just beginning to speed up the mail. Up to then, the mail had been carried by horse. Otherwise, there had been little change. Ships hoisted flags to signal to each other. Armies used semaphore—signals sent by placing the arms holding flags in different positions for

"I know that my fortune is in my own hands. I know that complete and perfect success is close at hand."

Bell, in a letter to his parents, October 1876

9

each letter. Both methods—which worked only in daylight and in good weather—were known to the ancient Greeks. The slowness of communication meant that people had to arrange meetings or visits away from home weeks in advance. And doing business at a distance was almost impossible.

Dots and Dashes

A number of inventors produced telegraph machines that allowed messages to be sent instantaneously through wires. It was an American, Samuel F. Morse, who invented the standard telegraph, the machine that was finally adopted. The invention was based on the electromagnet. This is a piece of iron with a coil of wire around it. When an electric current flows through the wire, the iron becomes magnetized and, like all magnets, attracts iron. When the current is switched off, the magnet effect stops.

The main London telegraph office in 1871.

Morse also invented a code of dots and dashes to represent letters of the alphabet. To send a telegraph message, the operator tapped out the words in Morse code. When the operator pressed the key of the transmitter, an electrical circuit was completed and a burst of current went down the wire to the receiver. This magnetized an electromagnet, which attracted an iron pin. When the pin hit the electromagnet, it made a sharp tap. The operator at the receiving end translated the short taps ("dots") and long taps ("dashes") back into the words of the message, or the taps were marked with a pencil on a moving reel of paper.

By using different arrangements of dots and dashes, Morse code covered all the letters of the alphabet, all the numerals from zero to nine, and even punctuation. The famous Morse code message was the emergency signal SOS—three dots (S) followed by three dashes (O) followed by three dots (S). On a paper tape it would come out like this: "...---..."

In 1844, Morse set up the first public telegraph system, covering the 37 miles between New York and Baltimore. Soon, telegraph companies were operating between all the main towns and cities of the East coast. In the late 1860s, after the Civil War ended, the rail network pushed westward across the United States, and telegraph lines ran alongside. Soon, every trading post and station had its own telegraph office to send and receive messages.

A Pricey Message

The telegraph was a much faster means of communication than anything that had been known before, but it had drawbacks. If you wanted to send a telegram, you had to go to the telegraph office. The message itself, in the "dots" and "dashes" of Morse code, arrived quickly, but at the

*Nineteenth-century
Edinburgh, where
Alexander Graham
Bell was born in 1847.*

receiving end it had either to be delivered to or col-
lected by the recipient. If there was a reply, this
lengthy procedure had to be performed in reverse.

Although the technology of the telegraph was
fairly simple, making use of it as a means of communication was expensive. It needed a network of
offices, all linked by lines, staffed around the clock.
Landowners demanded fees to run lines over their
land, and it was costly to put up the lines.

Once up, the lines had to be maintained. Only
the largest companies could set up an efficient network. In the United States two companies,
Western Union and the Atlantic and Pacific
Telegraph Company, dominated the telegraphy
business.

Sending a telegram was costly compared to a letter. For this reason, private telegrams tended to be
restricted to urgent messages. For many people,
telegrams were associated with bad news.

A Boon to Business

Despite its drawbacks, the telegraph was a great boon to businesses, especially to those with their own telegraph offices. The telegraph also made it possible to schedule and signal trains to safety and to transmit news reports quickly. By 1870, the first undersea cables had been laid in the Atlantic Ocean, and there was direct communication by telegraph between North America and Europe.

Both the Western Union and the Atlantic and Pacific Telegraph Company had invested heavily in setting up their networks. They were both looking forward to huge profits. This was why the news of a "speaking telegraph" was so unwelcome to the telegraph companies, especially Western Union.

Migrants from Scotland

At the age of twenty-three, Alexander Graham Bell arrived in North America from Scotland. It was

The mid-to-late 1800s— when Bell and his family left their homeland—was a period of large-scale immigration to America. This painting shows a typical scene at dockside, before an emigrant ship set sail.

13

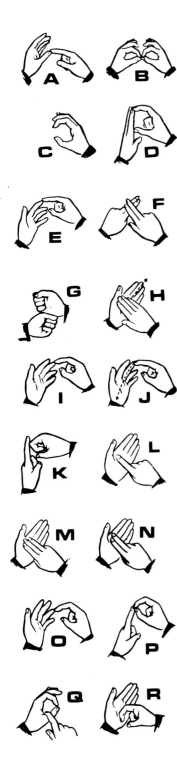

1870, just as the development of the telegraph was reaching its peak.

It was an exciting time to be in America. In 1869, the Union Pacific and Central Pacific railroads had met in Promontory, Utah, completing the first transcontinental rail link. This transportation milestone marked the beginning of America's expansion into the Midwest. With the Civil War behind it, American industry was booming, turning its efforts to the production of profitable peacetime products. A steady influx of immigrants provided a huge, hungry workforce for America's factories.

Bell's father and grandfather were both teachers of elocution. They provided speech therapy, trying to cure such problems as stuttering. Bell's father had developed a system of writing that he called "Visible Speech." The language was based on symbols that showed how the lips and tongue should be arranged to make particular sounds. Bell's father, also named Alexander, was immersed in his work with Visible Speech. He had a dominating personality and insisted that his three sons learn Visible Speech and take part in demonstrating it. There was some interest in Visible Speech among elocution teachers, but Alexander Sr. was disappointed when he tried to persuade the British government to recommend it for all state schools. In 1868, he had been on a lecture tour of the United States hoping to find some interest there.

Children in a Silent World

Bell's father was interested in the problems of people he called "deaf mutes"—children and adults who had been born deaf or had gone deaf at such a young age that they had little or no experience of hearing speech. He thought that Visible Speech could help them.

Family Tragedy

Alexander Graham Bell ("Graham" was actually an additional name that he chose for himself as a schoolboy) was born on March 3, 1847, the second of three sons. His brother, Melville, was two years older. His brother, Edward, was a year younger. Both brothers died of tuberculosis as young men, within three years of each other. This tragedy led the Bell family to move to North America. There, they hoped, the environment would be healthier—for Alexander had never been very strong, and the opportunities for his father's Visible Speech would be even greater.

Out of Father's Shadow

Young Alexander did not want to go to America. He was teaching at a school for the deaf in London, using Visible Speech among other methods. He had also started a degree course at London University. He had found someone he wished to marry, and was only waiting for the opportunity to propose to her. Above all, he wanted to make his own life, out of his father's shadow.

Alexander Sr. was a domineering nineteenth-century father. He expected his son to do exactly what he was told—even to marry a woman with his family's approval. Alexander Sr. had expected all three of his sons to follow him into the family "business" of speech training. He had denied them independence by refusing them money unless they asked for, and accounted for, every penny.

To Canada

As the only surviving son, young Alexander felt it was his duty to go with his parents, although it lessened his chances of breaking free of his father's influence. After a long night trying to make up his mind, Alexander decided that he could not leave

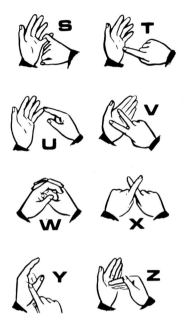

Opposite and above: *The two-handed alphabet used to communicate in sign language.*

When Bell arrived in Boston in 1871, it was a bustling center of commerce with a thriving seaport. It was also abuzz with cultural and scientific activity.

his parents forever. He abandoned his studies, wrote a final sad letter to his girlfriend, and on July 21, 1870, sailed with his parents for Quebec.

Alexander watched from the ship as the English coast slipped slowly out of sight. All his sadness made him feel that he had failed. At twenty-three, what had he achieved? He was still treated like a child in his father's household. He had been virtually forced into a career as a teacher of the deaf. And he even depended on his father's contacts for work. He had passed up some opportunities to gain other experience, and he did not pursue the marriage and independence he longed for in London. All Alexander saw in front of him was an uncertain future.

A New Life

Alexander Sr. was right in his hunch that America would be a more welcoming environment for Visible Speech. Inspired by one of the senior Bell's 1868 lectures, a teacher named Sarah Fuller had started a new school for the deaf in Boston. When Sarah found out that Bell was in America again, she got in touch with him. By the spring of 1871, young Alexander left his home in Brantford, Canada, and moved to Boston, where he began teaching at Sarah Fuller's Boston School for Deaf Mutes.

The Lure of Boston

Boston was, and still is, one of America's most cultured cities. In the mid-nineteenth century, its public library was the largest in America. In 1866, the world-famous Massachusetts Institute of Technology (M.I.T.) had been founded there. The city was at the heart of art, music, and cultural activities. It was an ideal home for a young man like Alexander, who had a broad set of interests and an insatiable curiosity. Excited and inspired by Boston's vibrancy, he was energized by his new life. Handsome, witty, and a very good pianist, he quickly became a welcome guest at elite Boston dinner parties.

Away from his father's control, Bell's commitment to teaching the deaf also became stronger in Boston. During this time, he not only used Visible Speech, but also developed some of his own experimental ways to teach deaf children and adults.

"My feelings and sympathies are every day more and more aroused," he wrote to his parents. "It makes my heart ache to see the difficulties the little children have to contend with."

The Patient Teacher

As a teacher, Bell was patient with his students. He explained how vibrations made sound waves, which, in turn, produced vibrations in the ears of people with normal hearing. He asked children to hold a balloon while he spoke with his lips against it so that they could feel the vibrations. He placed the children's hands on his larynx so they could feel the vibrations of his vocal cords as he made different sounds. In this way, they learned to distinguish between pairs of sounds that are very similar, such as "p" and "b". He convinced children who had never heard a sound that they, too, could learn to speak and make themselves understood.

His success with his young students was remarkable, and his fame as a teacher of the deaf quickly spread far beyond Boston.

A Wealthy Ally

As one of Boston's most celebrated teachers, Bell was introduced to a wealthy lawyer and business-man named Gardiner Greene Hubbard.

Hubbard had made a fortune from the growing rail network and from water and gas supplies. He was a successful lawyer, a Massachusetts senator, and a keen businessman. Only one thing caused him serious worry. Of his three children, only his daughter Mabel had survived infancy. And when Mabel was five, she had become totally deaf as a result of scarlet fever. The only words she could speak were the few she had learned as a toddler, and even these had become distorted and hard to understand.

Hubbard used his considerable wealth and influence to obtain the best education for Mabel. He was determined that she should learn to speak

Alexander Graham Bell is at the top right of this group photograph taken at the Boston School for the Deaf in June 1871.

19

"normally." He hired a governess for Mabel, sent his daughter to a special school in Germany, and even opened a school near his home for her. Because Mabel was very intelligent, she excelled at her schoolwork and became an expert lip reader. However, her speech remained poor.

In 1873, Bell was appointed professor of speech and elocution at Boston University's School of Oratory. This was a tremendous compliment and an acknowledgment of his success at Sarah Fuller's school. Among the people who came to see him at the university was Mabel Hubbard, now fifteen. Bell agreed to take her on as a pupil and to try to improve her speech with some of his methods.

Sign versus Speech

Both Bell's appointment to the School of Oratory and Hubbard's choice of him as Mabel's teacher were a tribute to his particular method of teaching.

There were—and still are—two basic methods of teaching deaf people to communicate. One is to use sign language, spelling out words and ideas with the fingers in a kind of code. There are many versions of sign, but the version most often used was developed in France in the eighteenth century. It evolved from a language of deaf people in Paris who had developed the system for themselves. Sign enables deaf people to communicate with each other and with others who have learned it. Critics of sign, such as Bell and his father, argued that it limits deaf people to communicating mostly with other deaf people.

Visible Speech was an attempt to improve on sign by teaching deaf people to form vowels and consonants and thus to be able to communicate more freely with "normal hearing" individuals. This approach was one of a number of techniques known as the "oral method."

"I think I can be of far more use as a teacher of the deaf than I can ever be as an electrician."

Alexander, writing to Mabel, 1878

The argument between those who preferred sign and those who preferred the oral method divided teachers of the deaf. The oral-method teachers argued that deaf children should be taught to live as normally as possible in the world of the hearing. Sign language, these oral teachers said, condemned deaf children to live as second-class citizens in a prison of silence. Not so, argued the pro-sign teachers. They believed sign enabled those who had learned it to communicate better and more deeply. Learning the oral method, they said, was a huge undertaking that limited a pupil's vocabulary and ability to express ideas.

There was still another angle to the argument. Many deaf children had been taught to speak, but their speech sounded so different that they sounded like they had learning difficulties. In the

Mabel Gardiner Hubbard, at about six years old. A year earlier, she had contracted scarlet fever.

nineteenth century, many people felt that it was better for a child to be "mute" than to be thought of as "mentally defective."

Bell's methods helped to change concerns about speaking by showing children how sounds were made and by improving the quality of his pupils' speech. The "sign or sound" argument is still going on today. Many therapists who believe in sign still blame Bell for having popularized the "oral method."

The Spare-time Scientist

Busy as he was, Bell still enjoyed the hobby of scientific experiments. He found that telegraphy was both exciting and accessible. It needed little equipment, and the few things he needed were easily obtainable or could be made at home. As a part-time inventor, Bell learned about some of the most interesting new technology of the time. Though telegraph equipment was still in its infancy, there was always the possibility—or at least the dream—of accidentally coming across a profitable breakthrough. In the early days of radio, many enthusiasts were attracted to this hobby for similar reasons.

Bell had always been interested in the telegraph. When he was still in his teens, he and a friend had rigged up a wire between their houses over which they exchanged messages in code. Using what he knew about sound from his father, young Bell had also experimented by combining that knowledge with what he knew of telegraphy.

Bell was interested in how the human mouth could make so many different sounds, and in particular how vowels were formed. Experimenting with a tuning fork held in front of his mouth, he found that the movement of his tongue, as he formed it for different vowel sounds, altered the pitch of the fork. Through these experiments, Bell learned that vowel sounds were related to pitch.

This discovery had already been made by a German scientist, Hermann Helmholtz, who had made an apparatus to sound tuning forks to required pitches by means of electricity. A friend translated Helmholtz's account of his work for Bell, and although he did not fully understand it, he grasped the basic idea—that electricity could be used to generate sounds of different pitches and values. This was progress over the telegraph, which offered only sound or silence, according to whether the current was flowing from the sender or not. There was a long way to go between Helmholtz's apparatus and the telephone, but already, by the time he was nineteen, Bell had taken the first step. His first thought was that he might be able to use the power of electricity to generate different pitches of sound. He also realized that this idea could potentially help deaf people.

In addition to his work with the telephone, Bell played a part in the beginnings of sound recording. He certainly would have been delighted to know that today people with severe speech difficulties are able to speak with the help of synthesizers—microcomputers that use electricity to generate sound.

The Telegraph Falls Short

It was a problem that the early telegraph could only send one message at a time. When demand was high, this caused delays and defeated the telegraph's aim of rapid and instant communication. Busy telegraph offices were often full of people waiting to send or receive messages. For example, someone behind a news reporter with a long article to send was in for a very long wait.

The problem was particularly frustrating for the telegraph companies. They saw that if they could

"When people can order everything they want from the store without leaving home and chat comfortably with each other by telegraph over some piece of gossip, every person will desire to put money in our pockets by having telephones."

Alexander, in a letter to Mabel, November 1876

23

increase the capacity of their lines, they would be able to do a lot more business. There was a rich reward waiting for the inventor who could come up with a way to ease this problem. It was into this race that, almost by accident, Alexander Graham Bell stumbled.

The Harmonic Telegraph

By 1872, telegraph companies were installing an improvement—the duplex system. This allowed one message to be sent in each direction at the same time, but it could not help if, for example, there were numerous messages waiting to be sent in one direction. Thinking about this, Alexander Graham Bell recalled Helmholtz's experiments and his own, and had the idea of a "harmonic telegraph." If electricity could generate different pitches of sound, wouldn't it be possible to send a mixture of pitches—each carrying a different message—over a wire at the same time and be "unscrambled" at the receiving end?

It was still in Bell's mind that the electrical production of different pitches could in some way help his deaf pupils, but he became more and more interested in applying the idea to the telegraph. During the winter of 1872-73, the twenty-five-year-old Bell began to work seriously

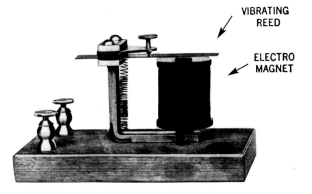

VIBRATING
REED

ELECTRO
MAGNET

This is a replica of the "harmonic telegraph" instruments that Alexander Graham Bell and Thomas Watson used for their historic breakthrough in June 1875.

24

on a harmonic telegraph project. He experimented, often through the night, and mostly in secret. He was very wary about discussing his ideas with anyone else, for fear that someone would use the information to develop an invention first. He read as much electrical theory as he could, but had little experience with electricity. Working by trial and error offered him little success.

This was the stage he had reached when, in 1873, he was offered a professorship at Boston University. When he accepted the post, he put his experiments aside.

By the following winter, Bell had managed to find the time to make a harmonic telegraph that sent simultaneous signals on two different pitches.

Alexander in Love

As his experiments progressed, Bell's mind became increasingly fixed on a distinctly non-scientific matter. He was falling in love with one of his pupils, sixteen-year-old Mabel Hubbard. For nearly two years, he kept this to himself. He was ten years older than Mabel, and her father, a wealthy and powerful man, might not be keen for his daughter to marry a university professor. Even if Mabel accepted Bell's proposal, it seemed unlikely that her father and mother would.

"I know I am not much of a woman yet, but I feel very much what this is to have as it were my whole future life in my hands.... Of course it cannot be, however clever and smart Mr. Bell may be; and however much honored I should be by being his wife I never could love him or even like him thoroughly....If Mr. Bell does ask me, I shall not feel as if he did it through love. You need not write about my accepting or declining his offer if it should be made. I would do anything rather than that."

Mabel Hubbard, in a letter to her mother, July 1875

One thing about Bell did endear him to Gardiner Greene Hubbard. The millionaire, it turned out, was also interested in telegraphy and in ways of increasing the capacity of telegraph lines for business purposes.

Hubbard's Plan

Hubbard had some reservations about the Western Union Telegraph Company. He accused Western Union of holding back progress in telegraphy so that it could continue to demand high prices for telegrams. The answer, he said, was to set up a rival service that made use of the new technology. He also proposed to use post offices as stations where telegrams could be sent and received. Hubbard thought that this would halve the cost of sending telegrams and make them almost as cheap as letters.

Alexander Graham Bell (right) and Thomas Watson in the Exeter Place laboratory in Boston, which was financed by Gardiner Greene Hubbard and his partner Thomas Sanders.

This was Hubbard's argument. The truth was that Hubbard had spent most of his business life building up service industries like water and gas supplies, and telegraphy was another such industry with profits he wanted to share. The only way of breaking the power of the two telegraph giants was to find a more economical way of operating a telegraph system. When Bell told him about his experiments with the harmonic telegraph, Hubbard was convinced that it was the key to setting up a rival telegraph service.

A crisis was now brewing in Bell's life. He enjoyed his work at the university and his private teaching, especially when Mabel Hubbard was his pupil. But he was becoming more interested in his work on the harmonic telegraph. His sense of urgency was increased when he heard that Elisha Gray was also working on similar projects.

Gray had limitless time in which to pursue his experiments. Bell had to fit his experiments in with a busy academic and professional life. If Bell had known that Edison was also at work in the same field, funded by the mighty Western Union, Bell's confidence would surely have been shaken.

At this point, Gardiner Greene Hubbard made Bell an offer. Hubbard would fund Bell's experiments in return for a share of the profit—if Bell managed to register his patent first. He would also organize the patent application. The father of another one of Bell's pupils, Thomas Sanders, also agreed to put up some money. It looked as if Bell could actually join the invention race. All he had to do was beat Edison and Gray.

"A Neck and Neck Race"

By November 1874, Bell knew he and Gray were progressing equally. "It is a neck and neck race between Mr. Gray and myself who shall complete

> "If I succeed in securing the Patent without interference from the others, the whole thing is mine and I am sure of fame, fortune, and success if I can only persevere in perfecting my apparatus."
>
> Bell, in a letter to his father, February 1876

the apparatus first," he wrote. Assessing his chances, he thought that Gray had an advantage with his knowledge of electricity, but that he [Bell] knew more about the science of sound.

Hubbard's and Sander's financial support enabled Bell to hire a part-time assistant and rent a workshop in Boston. The assistant was twenty-year-old Thomas Watson. The decision to employ him was one that Bell made reluctantly. He was, by nature, someone who preferred to work on his own, and he was also worried about his secrets leaking out.

But Watson was the perfect choice. He was as enthusiastic as Bell, as prepared to work long hours, and as determined not to even think about the possibility of failure. Best of all, he was a skilled electrician who made up for the gaps in Bell's own knowledge.

By the spring of 1875, Bell and Watson had developed the harmonic telegraph to the point where it was ready to be registered at the Patent Office. It was still not reliable, and endless adjustments would be needed, but both men were satisfied that the principle was right.

Breakthrough

An ordinary telegraph receiver responded to any burst of electrical current sent along the wire. The principle of Bell's harmonic telegraph was that the transmitter and receiver had a number of steel reeds, each tuned to a different pitch in pairs. Messages could be sent between each pair of reeds at the same time, but a reed in the receiver would respond only when the transmitter reed with the same pitch was used to transmit current. The pitches chosen for the reeds had to be far enough apart to avoid the possibility of a receiver reed responding to more than one transmitter reed.

On June 2, 1875, Bell and Watson were working on the apparatus when one of the three sets of transmitters and receivers developed a fault. It did not transmit its pitched note. Bell was in the transmitter room, and he went through to ask Watson to switch off the current in the receiver room.

By the time Watson had found the faulty reed, Bell was back with transmitters. When Watson flicked the sticking reed free, the reed of Bell's transmitter vibrated enough to give an audible sound. The vibration caused by Watson's fingers prying the jammed reed free had been transmitted to Bell's apparatus in the other room.

Was it a breakthrough, or a mere accident?

Bell and Watson changed places and tried again. Again they had the same result. The meaning of this was clear: Sound itself could be transmitted in electrical form, and it could be translated back into

Bell's laboratory notebooks were filled with hastily sketched diagrams like those shown here.

sound at the other end. But what was even more remarkable was that this had happened when the electrical current had been switched off. Bell and Watson reasoned that a small amount of the magnetism had been left in the electromagnet when it was switched off, and it was this that had made the reeds vibrate and sound. The fault in the apparatus that afternoon had turned the dream of the "speaking telegraph," or telephone, into reality. It was only the beginning, but that day the telephone was born.

Backing Two Horses

Bell, who was already overworked, now had two major projects to cope with—the harmonic telegraph and the telephone. Hubbard wanted Bell to concentrate on the telegraph, which seemed more likely to have commercial possibilities.

Bell's love for Mabel Hubbard was known by now in the Hubbard household, and Mabel had revised her opinion of him a little. She did not love him yet, she told him, but she no longer disliked him. Bell started to court Mabel seriously. He was encouraged by Mabel's mother, who had always liked him.

Now, Mabel's father hinted to Bell that only the profits from the harmonic telegraph would provide enough money for the young man to marry her. To Bell, this sounded like blackmail, and he reacted angrily. For a few days, the partnership hung in the balance. (If they had parted company at this point, it is likely that Elisha Gray would have gone down in history as the inventor of the telephone.) Eventually, Hubbard and Bell cooled down, and Bell continued to work on both projects.

Engaged

On Thanksgiving Day in 1875, Mabel's eighteenth birthday, she and Bell became engaged. When the public holiday was over, he returned to his work.

By this time, Bell had already succeeded in sending a sound of a particular frequency over a wire, but he knew that there was a big gap between this and sending speech.

The sound of a human voice is made up of a whole range of sound waves. These waves vibrate at different rates called frequencies. Different people's voices use different parts of this range. For example, children's and women's voices are higher than men's. All human voices fall within the range of frequencies that the human ear can hear.

If the telephone was going to be able to carry a human voice, Bell realized, it must be able to transmit and receive a wide range of frequencies. It was not necessary to transmit every one of the frequencies. Even modern telephones don't do this (they cut off the top and bottom frequencies). This is why some familiar voices may sound different, and why sometimes it is hard to recognize the voice of someone you know quite well on the telephone.

How to Change Frequencies

How could a large number of different frequencies be turned into changes in an electrical current? And how could the current be changed back again into sound frequencies at the receiving end? To find the answer, Bell's thoughts turned to what he had learned. As a teacher of the deaf, he knew a good deal about how the voice and ear work.

The sound of speech is produced by vibrations of the vocal cords in our throats. The sound waves travel through the air to the listener's ear. They produce identical vibrations in a part of the ear called the eardrum. This is a thin, tightly stretched piece of skin called a membrane. The vibrations of the membrane are picked up by the nerves in the ear and then transmitted to the brain.

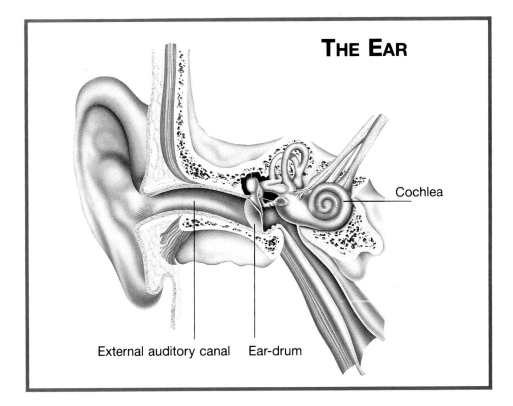

THE EAR

Cochlea

External auditory canal   Ear-drum

Bell used the workings of the human ear as his model for the telephone.

Was there, Bell wondered, a way to copy the vibrations of the vocal cords and the eardrum so that the wide range of frequencies produced by the human voice could be effectively sent on a wire as a series of electrical signals?

Imitating the Eardrum

Bell decided that the answer was to imitate the membrane of the ear with a device called a diaphragm. This was a sheet of material thin enough to vibrate from the sound of the voice, and in response to small changes in electrical current. Attached to the middle was a magnetized reed, which moved when the diaphragm moved. The reed moved inside an electromagnet and as it did, the sound vibrations were turned into changes in current. These changes in current went along the

"I am afraid to go to sleep lest I should find it all a dream, so I shall lie awake and think of you."

Alexander, in a letter to Mabel after their engagement, November 1875

wire to the receiver. There, they made the receiver's diaphragm vibrate, changing the signals back into the original sound.

On July 1, 1875, Bell tried out his new diaphragm telephone for the first time by singing into it. Watson, listening on the receiver in the next room heard him.

For a time, Bell's work on the harmonic telegraph and the telephone went on side by side. Hubbard still urged him to spend more time on the telegraph, so Bell and Watson had to "steal" time to work on the telephone. As 1876 began, both Bell and Watson were close to nervous exhaustion from overwork. Even so, they managed to draw up the telephone patent application, which Hubbard took to Washington in mid-February.

Still a Challenge

Returning to Boston with the patent for the telephone, Bell was, of course, overjoyed. But he knew that the granting of a patent was just the first step. His patent contained only a description of how he proposed to set about making a telephone. Bell had yet to actually make a device that worked.

By March 8, the day after he returned from Washington, he and Watson were hard at work in the laboratory, which was above a restaurant. Bell slept in one room and worked in the other. For quick meals, he went downstairs to the restaurant.

"Watson, Come Here"

Two days later, Watson listened on his receiver in Bell's bedroom while Bell spoke into the transmitter. Bell wrote a detailed account of what happened next in his laboratory notebook.

Bell shouted into the mouthpiece of the transmitter the words "Mr. Watson, come here.

Above: *March 9, 1876: Watson (right) rushed into the laboratory and told Bell that he had heard Bell calling him.*

Opposite: *A studio portrait of Bell taken in the 1870s.*

I want to see you." Watson rushed through and said that he had heard and understood the message. Bell asked him to repeat it, and he did so. Then they changed places and Bell listened while Watson read from a book. The results were not quite so good. "The effect was loud but indistinct and muffled," wrote Bell, "but an occasional word here and there was quite distinct. Finally the sentence 'Mr. Bell, do you understand what I say?' came quite clear and intelligibly."

Improvements and Variations

Bursting with excitement, Bell and Watson took turns sending messages to each other. "How do

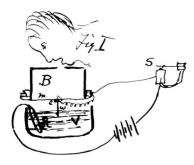

Alexander's sketch of his first successful harmonic telegraph, from the entry in his laboratory notebook on March 9, 1876.

you do?" they asked each other. Bell sang a verse of the British national anthem. Hubbard was invited to Exeter Place to hear the telephone in use. A few days later, Bell's father came to experience the miracle. Day after day, Bell and Watson tried out new ideas, new variations, and new improvements. The results became more and more reliable.

It was enormously exciting for Bell and Watson to be a part of creating this new technology. Each small new improvement seemed to them to be a great leap forward. Of course, compared to modern telephones, Bell's apparatus was quite primitive. The speaker had to shout into the mouthpiece, and the listener would—with luck—hear a faint, distorted sound at the other end, often accompanied by cracklings and rustlings. The most difficult obstacles, however, had been overcome. Now, it was a matter of refining and improving.

Along with all this excitement, Bell was still a full-time professor at Boston University. He had lectures, class lists, and exam papers to think about. He was also writing daily to his young fiancé, Mabel Hubbard.

Health Problems

How did Bell manage to do so much each day? The answer was that he had gotten into the habit of working through the night, free from interruption, until about 4:00 A.M. Only at that point would he sleep until mid-morning. These erratic hours, combined with rushed meals, dashing to his lecture hall and back again to the laboratory, all affected Bell's health.

The inventor was faced with yet another challenge. He needed to convince people—the right people—of all the things his telephone could do.

"I often feel as if I shall go mad with the feverish anxiety of my unsettled life. I do so long to have a home of my own, with you to share it."

Alexander, in a letter to Mabel, April 1877

Outside the handful of scientists and inventors, the telephone was virtually unknown—and to any ordinary person who heard about it, the telephone sounded like something from science fiction. If the invention was ever to succeed and take hold, Bell and Hubbard needed to enlist a whole group of powerful and wealthy investors for help.

There were still other issues. Who was going to put up the money for lines, for the telephones themselves, and for the exchanges or connecting offices? Was the telephone really going to be an improvement in the quality of life, or was it, as Hubbard had believed, only an interesting toy?

Fear of the Telephone

Then there were the worries, fueled by some newspapers—and perhaps by Western Union, which wanted to hold on to its telegraph business. Would having the telephone be like letting a spy into your house? Would everyone else on the line be able to hear what you were saying? If electricity could carry voices down the line, could it also carry disease? Could the telephone actually hurt you? Could it make people go deaf or even mad?

No scientist or business leader took these worries seriously, but they needed to be addressed if a nationwide telephone system was to be created. So Bell added to his work a publicity campaign designed to make the telephone publicly acceptable. He knew that it was important for him to get his name in the newspapers and have his ideas discussed openly. Luckily, he was an impressive and experienced public speaker, and, like many good teachers, also had a touch of showmanship.

One of his first "stunts," designed to get people talking, was performed at a meeting in May 1876 of the American Academy of Arts and Sciences.

. . . .

"The telephone is mixed up in a most curious way in my thought with you. Even in its present condition I think the instrument can be made a commercial success—so I give you fair warning that it won't be long before I claim a certain promise—oh! I forgot! It was I that made the promise and not you! However I shall claim it all the same!"

Alexander, writing to Mabel, November 1876

. . . .

The Centennial Exhibition grounds in Philadelphia, 1876, with the exhibition halls in the background.

At the meeting, Bell pressed a key on his lectern. The audience was amazed to hear, from a box on the table, the tune of a hymn.

In a building along the street, Mabel's cousin, William, was playing a "telegraphic organ." Its keys were linked by telegraph line to the box in the lecture hall. The organ transmitted each note, on its particular frequency, to tuned reeds in the box. These reeds responded to the signals and played the tune.

The staid academic audience went wild with admiration—and Bell got his name into the papers. In truth, what he had demonstrated was not the

telephone but an ingenious application of the principle of his harmonic telegraph. Nonetheless, his mission was accomplished.

A Surprise for the Emperor

A great opportunity for publicity came with the Centennial Exhibition in Philadelphia in 1876. Exhibitions of trade and industry were popular in the second half of the nineteenth century. They enabled manufacturers to show off their latest wares, and visitors to see what new goods were available. They were also showplaces for new "cutting-edge" inventions, and the exhibition organizers awarded medals for the most promising exhibits. For the United States, the Centennial Exhibition was particularly important. It was intended to show the rest of the world that America was a world leader in innovation and technology.

What happened at the Centennial Exhibition became, in Bell's old age, one of his most repeated stories. The exhibition was closed to the public on Sundays, but on June 25, it was opened to admit a special party of distinguished visitors. The party included a number of American scientists, together with Emperor Pedro II of Brazil and a leading Scottish scientist, Sir William Thomson (later Lord Kelvin).

According to Bell's memory, the visitors proceeded slowly around the hall and spent a great deal of time at Elisha Gray's exhibit. The visitors were about to call it a day when they were persuaded to see Bell's demonstration.

"Among all these inventions, there was one which not only contributed most to the fame of the [Centennial] Exhibition, but established the name of the United States as a nation of brilliant inventors. Yet it was merely a simple device which its inventor, Alexander Graham Bell, publicly presented there for the first time under the name of 'telephone'.... When it became known that the telephone could speak, almost as perfectly as the human mouth, rendering the spoken words audibly even at a considerable distance, its fame spread like wildfire."

From the Dutch scientific journal, De Natuur, 1876

"I Hear, I Hear"

Bell's exhibit included his harmonic telegraph and also a telephone receiver. Wires ran to the transmitters about 100 yards away. He had arranged a semicircle of chairs on which the visitors were invited to sit. After explaining and demonstrating the harmonic telegraph, Bell turned to the telephone receiver. Then, leaving Hubbard in charge of the exhibit, he went to the transmitter. Sir William Thomson was invited to put the receiver to his ear. To his amazement, he heard the first snatch of song and then Bell's voice asking him, "Do you understand what I say?"

The next to try the new marvel was the emperor of Brazil. For him, Bell recited the famous "To be or not to be" speech from Shakespeare's play, *Hamlet*. The emperor jumped up, astounded. "I hear, I hear!" he cried.

Then, as now, newspapers were eager to report

"Five minutes' conversation is about as much as thirty pages of letter paper, and infinitely more intelligible. All the boasted civilization of the nineteenth century has not been able to give us anything even remotely suggesting an equivalent for a chat over a quiet pipe."

Unidentified Scottish scientist, 1871

Distinguished visitors gather around Alexander Graham Bell's exhibit at Philadelphia.

the doings of royalty, and the emperor's astonishment was the big story in the next day's Philadelphia papers. But what pleased Bell most was the reaction of his fellow-Scot and fellow-scientist, Sir William Thomson. Sir William came back later with his wife for another demonstration. Thomson was so impressed that he became the "champion" for Bell's telephone in Britain.

The Challenge of Distance

The real test of the telephone's usefulness, however, was its ability to carry voices over very long distances, using telegraph wires. Bell now set out to extend its range. He and Watson exchanged conversations at distances of 2 miles (3.2 km), 5 miles (8 km), and 16 miles (25.6 km).

Although he was not business minded by nature, Bell was aware of the commercial rewards to be gained if the telephone became a serious and practical means of communication. Knowing its potential, Bell was impatient to achieve that goal.

News by Telephone

The public really woke up to the possibilities of the telephone in February 1877, when Bell—almost thirty years old—did a demonstration for an audience in Salem, Massachusetts. Watson was 14 miles (22.4 km) away, in Boston. They exchanged songs, conversation, and the first news report to be sent by telephone. This appeared in the *Boston Globe* the next day with the headline: "Sent by telephone. The First Newspaper Dispatch Sent by a Human Voice Over the Wires." The story was copied by other newspapers all over North America, and was reported in scientific journals in Europe.

Not everyone was enthusiastic. Defeated and

....

"As I placed my mouth to the instrument it seemed as if an electric thrill went through the audience, and that they recognized for the first time what was meant by the telephone."

Bell, describing the Salem demonstration, 1877

....

sour, Elisha Gray dismissed Bell's telephone. "It only creates interest in scientific circles," he wrote. The telephone, Gray believed, would never supersede the telegraph. Neither had he been impressed by the demonstration at the Philadelphia Exhibition. All he had heard, he said, was "a very faint, ghostly, ringing sort of a sound."

The telephone also excited the suspicions of the superstitious. For many people, hearing a voice without seeing a body was a complete novelty. To some, the voices coming from the telephone were uncanny, supernatural—even evil. One American newspaper suggested that the telephone was an instrument of the devil. It was not the first or last time that a new invention came up against opposition from closed minds.

"It is indeed difficult, hearing the sounds out of the mysterious box, to wholly resist the notion that the powers of darkness are somehow in league with it."

From a leading article in the Providence Press, 1877

This modern illustration depicts Bell's and Watson's experiments with the harmonic telegraph.

ERIC FRASER

GRAHAM BELL'S TELEPHONE 1876

PRO 149

Improvements

Although the technology was improving, the issue of design arose. The models that Bell had demonstrated were not simple or convenient enough for use by the masses. To send a message, Bell's models required a person to bellow into a box while standing on a table. Then, to hear the answer, one had to bend an ear close to the box. Bell designed improved models, but it was a design by another inventor, William Channing, that became the first telephone for general use. It was a one-piece instrument that was used alternately as a mouthpiece and an earpiece. This slowed up telephone conversations considerably and led to a great deal of confusion.

On April 4, 1877, an electrician for whom Watson had worked, Charles Williams, became the first person to be "on the telephone" on a permanent basis. A line connected his Boston shop with his home. Soon, more people wanted to have the new invention in their homes, but this raised a commercial question: Should customers rent their telephones or buy them outright? The eventual decision was to rent telephones, although this meant less money came immediately to Bell and his partners.

One telephone variation, demonstrated in late 1877, used separate listening and speaking instruments.

THE DAILY GRAPHIC

AN ILLUSTRATED EVENING NEWSPAPER.

39 & 41 PARK PLACE.

VOL. XIII. | All the News. Four Editions Daily. | NEW YORK. THURSDAY, MARCH 15, 1877. | $12 Per Year in Advance. Single Copies, Five Cents. | NO. 1246.

TERRORS OF THE TELEPHONE—THE ORATOR OF THE FUTURE.

45

Opposite: Telephone companies used ads like these to promote the use of the telephone.

This switchboard, made in Cincinnati, could take 50 lines. It was used in Drammen, Norway, from 1880 to 1889.

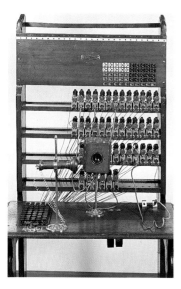

To get a real telephone system off the ground, Bell and his associates needed a network of lines. Negotiations with Western Union came to nothing. The giant of the telegraph industry was still anxious not to damage its telegraphy business or to hold up telegrams by sharing its lines with telephones.

In any case, as it turned out, the heavy telegraph lines were not suitable for the telephone. In July 1877, Bell, Watson, Hubbard, and Thomas Sanders (who had given Bell early financial backing) officially formed the Bell Telephone Company.

A week or so later, on July 11, Bell married Mabel Gardiner Hubbard. They sailed to Europe for an extended honeymoon, which included a demonstration of the telephone—by royal command—to Queen Victoria.

The Greatest Enemy

By the summer of 1878, the newspapers and scientific journals were printing exciting reports about the possibilities of the telephone. The French magazine, *La Nature*, had an account, with a picture, of a public telephone booth being used by the police to summon help for a man hurt in a traffic accident. Almost certainly, at that date, this was simply a publicity stunt. Many of the news stories about the telephone owed more to imagination than to fact, but this did not worry Bell, Hubbard, and Watson. Indeed, Bell was responsible for some of the fanciful ideas that appeared in the papers. As far as he was concerned, any publicity was good publicity.

Though there was no shortage of press coverage about the telephone, ·there was little enthusiasm among the public. People were less keen to sample the new communications miracle than its inventor had expected. By June 1878, only 100 telephones had been sold. By August there were 600, and by

the end of the year, there were a total of 2,600. No one could say that the telephone was taking North America by storm.

It was a similar story in the other countries where Bell had patented the telephone. His company's greatest enemy was public apathy—there was simply not enough interest. As is true when most innovations first become available, the public was cautious. Many were waiting for more improvements to be made. Others were waiting to see if the prices would go down.

New Haven Makes Telephone History

In the case of the telephone, there was good reason to wait for improvements. The first telephone lines ran between one place and another. An owner (or "subscriber," as someone who had a telephone was called) could speak only to another owner to whom the line was connected. There was no exchange system to connect a subscriber with a variety of others.

The first telephone exchange was opened in New Haven, Connecticut, in January 1878. Reception was still poor and there were frequent breakdowns. The lines suffered interference from nearby telegraph lines, and it was often necessary to shout a sentence three or four times before it was understood at the other end.

Many of these early problems had more to do with organizing the telephone system rather than with the invention itself. For the most part, these problems did not concern Bell. He admitted that he had little business flair. "Financial dealings," he once wrote, "are distasteful to me and not at all in my line." So he was happy to leave that side of the Bell Telephone business to Hubbard. This way, he could concentrate, at least for a while, on his demonstrations and lectures.

The New Haven District Telephone Company, in Connecticut, had the first telephone exchanges and was one of the first telephone directories. This directory took up only one side of a sheet of paper, and was not arranged in alphabetical order!

LIST OF SUBSCRIBERS.

New Haven District Telephone Company.

OFFICE 219 CHAPEL STREET.

February 21, 1878.

Residences.	*Stores, Factories, &c.*
Rev. JOHN E. TODD.	O. A. DORMAN.
J. B. CARRINGTON.	STONE & CHIDSEY.
H. B. BIGELOW.	NEW HAVEN FLOUR CO. State St.
C. W. SCRANTON.	" " " " Cong. ave.
GEORGE W. COY.	" " " " Grand St.
G. L. FERRIS.	" " " " Fair Haven.
H. P. FROST.	ENGLISH & MERSICK.
M. F. TYLER.	New Haven FOLDING CHAIR CO.
L. H. BROMLEY.	H. HOOKER & CO.
GEO. E. THOMPSON.	W. A. ENSIGN & SON.
WALTER LEWIS.	H. B. BIGELOW & CO.
	C. COWLES & CO.
Physicians.	C. S. MERSICK & CO.
Dr. E. L. R. THOMPSON.	SPENCER & MATTHEWS.
Dr. A. E. WINCHELL.	PAUL ROESSLER.
Dr. C. S. THOMSON, Fair Haven.	E. S. WHEELER & CO.
	ROLLING MILL CO.
Dentists.	APOTHECARIES HALL.
Dr. E. S. GAYLORD.	E. A. GESSNER.
Dr. R. F. BURWELL.	AMERICAN TEA CO.
Miscellaneous.	*Meat & Fish Markets.*
REGISTER PUBLISHING CO	W. H. HITCHINGS, City Market.
POLICE OFFICE.	GEO. E. LUM. " "
POST OFFICE.	A. FOOTE & CO.
MERCANTILE CLUB.	STRONG, HART & CO.
QUINNIPIAC CLUB.	
F. V. McDONALD, Yale News.	*Hack and Boarding Stables.*
SMEDLEY BROS. & CO.	CRITTENDEN & CARTER.
M. F. TYLER, Law Chambers.	BARKER & RANSOM.

Office open from 6 A. M. to 2 A. M.
After March 1st, this Office will be open all night.

"Sick of the Telephone"

There were many reasons that, by the late 1870s, Bell began to tire of his involvement with the telephone. First, business did not appeal to him, and he had no talent for it. Second, in 1878, Bell's right to call himself the inventor of the telephone was called into question. Accusations came from various sources, but the most damaging were those from Western Union and Elisha Gray. Bell was accused of having stolen Gray's ideas, and of dishonesty in his dealings with the Patent Office. These accusations, and court cases arising out of them, would go on for nearly twenty years. Bell eventually shrugged them off, but the first charges hurt him deeply. At one of his darkest moments, Bell wrote to Mabel, "I am sick of the telephone and have done with it altogether."

New Challenges

The truth was that Bell was not merely sick of the telephone, he was bored with it. He had made the great breakthrough. Then he let other people refine his idea, make improvements, set up systems, and sell the invention all over the world. Bell had a restless, curious, inquiring mind. It was this that led him to his great invention in the first place. Now that his income left him free to do as he pleased, he was ready to seek new challenges. "I must," he once told Mabel, "be accomplishing something."

Still Misunderstood

By 1880, the telephone was gaining significant popularity. That year, Bell was on a train in North Carolina when it broke down. The train conductor approached him, touching his cap.

"Excuse me, sir," said the conductor. "Are you the inventor of the telephone?"

"Yes," said Bell.

Boston was the birthplace of the telephone, and the site of the first telephone switchboard, in 1877.

"Do you happen to have a telephone with you?" asked the conductor. "We need to talk to the nearest stations and ask for help."

Bell had to explain that, even if he had a telephone in his pocket, the conductor's idea simply wasn't possible. It was an illustration of how the public had not completely understood the principle of how the telephone worked.

There was another story about a woman who went to her doctor. "The doctor's wife has gone mad," she reported to her husband later. "She had a box on the wall, and kept talking into it, pretending she was speaking to someone."

Another misconception regarding the telephone was that it might be responsible for transmitting diseases. The telephone reached Montreal, in Canada, at about the same time as an epidemic of smallpox. The disease was being spread, it was

Opposite: *Masses of telephone wires did nothing for the appearance of city skylines, especially in huge cities like New York.*

Below: *The main telephone exchange in Paris in 1904.*

said, down the telephone lines. It took a troop of soldiers to disperse the mob that gathered outside the telephone exchange.

Edison's Improvement

Steady improvements in the telephone system were being made every year. One of the most important improvements was made by Bell's old rival, Thomas Edison. Bell's diaphragm instrument acted well as a receiver, and an improved version is still used in almost all of the world's telephones today. But as a transmitter, it was less efficient. It had to be shouted at to pick up any sound at all, and the changes in current that it made were too feeble to be transmitted over long distances.

Edison worked on a transmitter in which the magnet was replaced by a small piece of carbon. He had discovered that if carbon were put under pressure—such as the pressure of sound waves—the flow of electricity through it was changed. The telephone transmitter, or mouthpiece, that he developed using this idea was basically the same as the one used today. The same principle was also used in the first microphones.

The changes in current produced by the carbon mouthpiece traveled better over long distances than those in Bell's diaphragm transmitter, but they needed to be boosted still further. They needed to be amplified for long distance calls. This led to Edison's second important contribution to the telephone: the induction coil. This coil was like a double electromagnet. Wires from the telephone mouthpiece led to an iron bar and were coiled around it. A second coil of wire, with more turns, was also wound around the bar, and then led to the telephone lines. In passing from the first coil to the second, the changes in electrical current were greatly amplified and could be carried over long distances.

A New Dial

Other inventors, as time went on, added further improvements to the telephone system. One of the most important of these inventors was not a scientist or an electrician, but an undertaker, Almon B. Strowger, who owned a small-town funeral business.

In the first telephone exchanges, callers were connected by hand to the lines of the people to which they wanted to speak. Callers turned a handle to alert the exchange operator, who then asked them which number they wanted. The operator then rang the number, and when there was an answer, they plugged the caller's line into the line of the other number. This took a little time, and there was also the worry that a nosy operator might listen to your conversation.

Strowger found the system more worrying than most other people. He worried that people who needed an undertaker would ring the exchange and would be put through to one of his rivals. So he worked on a system that would enable people to dial numbers for themselves. The Strowger automatic exchange, which he invented in 1889, enabled people to do just that. Each number on the dial admitted the caller to the next set of numbers, until the telephone with a particular number rang. Strowger's idea became the standard automatic system all over the world. It is still in use today, though it has been steadily replaced since the 1960s by electronic systems.

Slowly, telephone networks spread. A resident of Boston could, by 1884, easily talk to someone in New York. Chicago was hooked up for long distance calls in 1892, and Bell made the first call from New York. Yet it was not until 1915 that the east and west coasts of the United States were linked by telephone.

Opposite: In the first systems, each telephone was connected to the exchange by a separate wire, so huge structures like these were built.

Underground cables containing large numbers of lines replaced the old overhead system.

Even today, telephone lines play a major role in business and communication. These dealers on the Bourse, the Paris stock exchange, buy and sell shares by telephone.

Music by Phone

Soon after the telephone was invented, a *New York Times* writer dreamed that the telephone might someday be used to bring public events into the home. By the 1880s, this dream had become a reality. Even though the radio broadcasting of music was still about forty years away, a number of telephone companies in America and Europe began transmitting concerts and even plays over telephone lines. The theatrophone, as it was called, was briefly fashionable, although, according to one

report, "the sound produced by the telephones is generally so faint that it becomes necessary to oblige each listener to cover both ears with the telephones during the performance."

Many of the improvements that enabled the telephone to develop were the work of Bell's one-time rival, Thomas Edison. Bell was happy to let Edison refine the work he had begun. He was only concerned that his claim to have been the original inventor was upheld.

Bell bowed out of the telephone business in 1879, at age thirty-two, leaving the board of directors of the Bell Telephone Company. At about the same time, Thomas Watson also left. He, too, felt there were other things he wanted to do with his life. For people like Bell and Watson, the excitement of the telephone was over. Other people would get excitement out of building up the telephone business, but not them. Watson toured Europe, got married, and settled down as a farmer before launching into shipbuilding with great success. Bell, happily married and comfortably rich,

Top left: *The telephone brings communication to a village in the heart of Africa.*

Top right: *Telephone conversations are beamed across continents by satellite.*

Above: *Cables are still laid for shorter distances.*

55

moved to a new house in Washington and wondered what to do with the rest of his days.

Life in Washington

Mabel enjoyed the high society life of Washington, but Bell grew restless. He was in many ways a loner, and did not enjoy partaking in idle gossip. Much of Washington life revolved around dinner parties given to get the support of politicians for a cause—this, too, held no appeal for the inventor.

In his new-found fame, Bell did not forget his concern for deaf people. He founded a school for deaf children in Greenock, Scotland. In 1883, he opened another school in Washington, though it closed after two years because he could not find suitable teachers.

Prizes and medals came to Bell from all over the world. He was made a member of the French Legion d'Honneur. He became president of the National Geographic Society, which he helped to found, and regent of the Smithsonian Institution, one of the United States' leading scientific bodies. He was constantly in demand for lectures and articles.

A Need to Invent

Still, his mind could not rest. A sentence read by chance in the encyclopedia would set him off on a new train of thought, a new line of inquiry. He read the scientific journals and the newspapers keenly, keeping up to date with what other inventors were doing. Often, he would devise improvements for their ideas. The science fiction stories of the French writer Jules Verne now set Bell thinking about space travel and underwater exploration. Of course, it would be decades before any real technology in these areas would truly be possible.

Following the example of Edison, who had set

Bell was photographed here (on the right with white hair and beard) late in his life at a conference of teachers for the deaf in Tokyo, Japan.

up an "inventions laboratory," Bell built one of his own at Baddeck Bay in Nova Scotia, and another in Washington. Bell's reasoning was that he had invented the telephone in a makeshift laboratory above a restaurant, with just one assistant to help him. How much more fruitful it could be if he purposely built laboratories, properly staffed them, and gave them adequate funds to buy equipment! He was right: Over the next forty years, an astonishing variety of groundbreaking ideas came from these laboratories.

Edison had invented the induction coil to improve the telephone system and to make long distance calls possible. Now Bell was able to improve on one of Edison's inventions. This invention was the ancestor of today's record player, the phonograph, which recorded and played back sound on cylinders of tinfoil. Although it was hailed an ingenious, Edison's machine had little commercial value, except as a novelty. One problem was that the tinfoil cylinders wore out after only a few uses. In 1887, ten years after Edison, Bell developed a machine of his own, which he called the graphophone. This machine used longer-lasting cylinders made of hardened wax. The result was another fierce battle, this time with Edison, over patent rights. Ultimately, it was Bell's machine, with wax cylinders that could be played over and over again, that laid the foundations of modern sound recording.

The Light Telephone

One of the most promising ideas to come of Bell's later work was what he called the photophone. Late in his life, he was to describe it as his most important invention. This was a device for transmitting sound in beams of light, but Bell never succeeded in sending messages over a longer

"Wherever you may find the inventor, you may give him wealth or you may take away from him all that he had; and he will go on inventing. He can no more help inventing than he can help thinking or breathing."

Alexander Graham Bell, 1891

Opposite: *Today, wire cables are being replaced with optical strands— minute pieces of glass tube that carry laser-generated light signals. Bell experimented with a "light telephone," but his idea had to await the development of optics and laser technology to reach its full potential.*

Below: *Our present-day system of worldwide computer communication was built on a foundation of telephone technology.*

distance than 600 feet (183 m). The photophone is now regarded as the forerunner of modern optical communications that use laser light and glass strands—two technologies that were not available to Bell. While Bell was developing the photophone, an Italian scientist named Guglielmo Marconi was working on radio signals. He managed to transmit these signals for several miles while the photophone was working only in distances of feet.

So it was radio that became dominant in the field of communications during the early years of the twentieth century. For the rest of his life, however, Bell continued to believe in the possibilities of the photophone.

Bell also became fascinated with flying, and built countless kites. He test-ran hydrofoil speedboats, invented an air-conditioning system, and even developed a new breed of sheep. In the last year of his life, he was working on a portable system to take salt out of seawater, for use in lifeboats. And only a few months before he died, he took part in underwater explorations off the Bahamas.

Looking Back

In many ways, Bell's life after thirty was an attempt to recapture the excitement of his early days. His brain continued to buzz with ideas, but too often, these failed to turn into practical projects.

This was partly because his ideas outstripped available technology. Bell's excitable personality also led him to raise his own expectations—and those of others—too high. In his letters, his accounts of the early telephone experiments were exaggerated. Shortly after he received the telephone patent, for example, he told callers they would be able to see, as well as hear, their friends.

This excitability, combined with the hard-nosed commercial instinct of people like Hubbard, played a very important part in pushing the development of the telephone from a laboratory experiment to a working communications system that could be used worldwide.

Baddeck Bay was a refuge where Bell could combine the pursuit of his own personal scientific interests with a happy family life, emerging from time to time for a lecture tour or foreign travel. Meanwhile, he and his rival Edison worked into the twentieth century and became living monuments to an American spirit of inventiveness and ingenuity.

When he invented the telephone, Bell was a spare-time enthusiast with a full-time university job. Later in his life, when he was prosperous, he was still, at heart, an individual who was

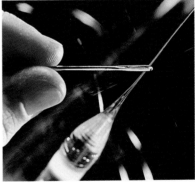

Above: *The future of the telephone depends on optical developments. Light signals can travel at a far greater speed than electrical pulses.*

interested mostly in ideas. Making money or gaining more fame interested him little.

Today, developments of comparable importance are usually the work of large, well-funded teams of people employed by huge companies or governments. It is unlikely that, in the future, an invention as significant as the telephone will be the work of one man working through the night, with little help and little money.

The Last Tribute

Bell lived long enough to see the start of the next important communications revolution. In the spring of 1922, shortly after his seventy-fifth birthday, he bought a radio and enjoyed listening to some of the first broadcast concerts and sports reports. He was still kept a notebook of ideas that sprang to his mind and of comments on what was happening at the Baddeck Bay laboratories.

By this time, the telephone had spread worldwide. The United States, with its need for business and private communication over long distances, was by far the world's most enthusiastic telephone market. By 1922, there were about 14 million telephones in the United States, or 1 for every 12 people—over half of all telephones in the world.

As usual, Alexander and Mabel Bell went to Baddeck Bay for the summer because Washington was too hot. Quite suddenly, near the end of July, Bell began to feel weak and lost his appetite. He died on August 2, 1922.

The funeral was held two days later at Baddeck Bay. As the service began, the telephone networks of Canada and the United States paid their own last tribute: For one minute, the entire system closed down. It was this special moment of silence that honored the man who had made those same wires first come alive with sound.

During his seventy-five years, Bell witnessed many milestones in science and technology. He is seen here with some of his grandchildren.

Important Dates

1847	March 3: Alexander Graham Bell is born in Edinburgh, Scotland.

1847   March 3: Alexander Graham Bell is born in Edinburgh, Scotland.

1858   Oct: Bell joins the Royal High School, Edinburgh.

1863   Aug: Aged sixteen, Bell begins teaching at Weston House school "for the Board and Education of Young Gentlemen," Elgin, Scotland.

1866   Sept: Bell, aged nineteen, takes up a teaching post at Somersetshire College, Bath.

1867   July: Bell joins his parents in London. Bell Sr. publishes his book on Visible Speech.

1868   May: Bell joins the staff of a private school in London.

Aug: Bell Sr. travels to the United States to demonstrate Visible Speech.

Oct: Bell begins studies at London University.

1870   May 18: Bell's brother, Melville, dies, aged twenty-three.

July 21: Bell and his parents leave for Canada.

1871   Apr 5: Bell joins the staff of the Boston School for Deaf Mutes.

1872   Apr 8: Bell meets Gardiner Greene Hubbard for the first time.

1873   Bell, aged twenty-four, is appointed professor of elocution at Boston University.

Mabel Hubbard first receives lessons from Bell as his private pupil.

Bell begins his experiments on a harmonic telegraph.

1874   Elisha Gray begins his experiments on a harmonic telegraph.

1875   Jan: With financial support from Gardiner Greene Hubbard and Thomas Sanders, Alexander employs Thomas Watson as his assistant.

Feb: Bell applies for a harmonic telegraph patent and signs a partnership agreement with Hubbard and Sanders.

June 2: The "sticking reed" in Bell's apparatus leads to experiments on the telephone.

1876   Feb: Bell's telephone patent application is presented and is approved on March 3.

March 10: Bell sends the world's first telephone message.

June 25: Bell demonstrates his telephone at the Centennial Exhibition in Philadelphia.

1877   Feb 12: Bell's Salem lecture attracts press attention.

July 9: The Bell Telephone Company is founded.

July 11: Bell marries Mabel Hubbard.

1878	May 8: Bell and Mabel's first daughter, Elsie, is born.
1879	Bell resigns from the Bell Telephone Company and founds a school for the deaf in Greenock, Scotland.
1880	Feb 15: Bell and Mabel's second daughter, Marian, is born.
	Sept: Bell is awarded the Volta Prize (for scientific achievement in electricity) in France and made an officer of the French Legion d'Honneur. With the prize money, he sets up the Volta Laboratory in Washington.
1881	Aug 15: Bell and Mabel's son, Edward, is born, but doesn't survive.
1883	Bell opens his own school for the deaf in Washington.
	Nov 17: The Bell's son, Robert, is born, but he doesn't survive.
1885	Nov: The Washington school for the deaf closes because of staffing problems.
1886	Bell buys a summer home at Baddeck Bay, Nova Scotia, and builds a laboratory there.
1887	Bell improves Edison's phonograph with his graphophone, the forerunner of the gramophone.
1890	Bell helps found the American Association for the Promotion of the Teaching of Speech to the Deaf and becomes its first president.
1898	Bell becomes president of the National Geographic Society and regent of the Smithsonian Institution.
1908	Bell starts his experiments with hydrofoils.
1911	Bell builds a hydrofoil, but it breaks up in trials.
1922	Aug 2: Bell Graham Bell dies, aged seventy-five.
1923	Jan 3: Mabel Bell dies.

For More Information

Books

Gearhart, Sarah. *The Telephone* (Turning Point Inventions). Old Tappan, NJ: Atheneum, 1999.

Lomask, Milton. *Invention and Technology* (Great Lives). Old Tappan, NJ: Atheneum, 1992.

Parker, Steve. *Alexander Graham Bell and the Telephone* (Science Discoveries). New York, NY: Chelsea House, 1995.

Turvey, Peter. *Inventions: Inventors and Ingenious Ideas* (Timelines). Danbury, CT: Franklin Watts, 1992.

Web Site

Bell's Lab Notebook—Read some of Bell's notes on various inventions in the inventor's own handwriting: Lcweb.loc.gov/exhibits/treasures/trr002.htm

Glossary

Amplify: To make stronger.

Audiometer: An instrument used to test human hearing.

Carbon: A naturally occurring chemical element of which coal and soot are made. The carbon used in Edison's first telephone mouthpiece was lampblack. It was used to replace the magnet in the transmitter.

Diaphragm: A thin piece of material stretched tightly across an opening. When the material is struck by a sound wave, it vibrates.

Dumb: A word that is condemned by many deaf people because, in addition to meaning mute, it can be used to mean "stupid."

Duplex: A system that allows messages to be sent in two directions at the same time, over the same wire.

Electromagnet: A magnet that is created when a coil of wire is wound around an iron core. The iron becomes magnetized when electricity flows through the wire.

Frequency: The number of times a sound wave vibrates in one second.

Hydrofoil: A type of ship with foils, or "wings," which skims the surface of the water.

Interference: Noises on a telephone line (or radio) caused by poor connections or other faults.

Larynx: The part of the throat that contains the vocal cords.

Mute: Silent or unable to speak.

Patent: The document granting an inventor the right to make, use, and sell an invention for a limited period of time.

Phonograph: The first machine for playing back recorded sound invented by Thomas Edison in 1877. Bell improved it by replacing the tinfoil cylinders with wax ones. This transformed the machine into the successful and popular forerunner of the gramophone.

Pitch: The quality of sound. It is determined by frequency, intensity, and loudness.

Receiver: A device that receives electromagnetic or electrical signals and converts them into an understandable form.

Soundwave: A pressure wave that travels through the air at about 1,000 feet (300 m) per second. As the wave moves, it creates a disturbance in the air pressure. This disturbance alternates between high and low pressure and is passed from one layer of air to the next. Sound waves can also travel through solids and liquids.

Telegram: A message sent by wire and delivered to the recipient by hand.

Transmitter: In a telephone, the part that converts sound waves into electrical signals.

Tuning fork: A metal fork that produces a musical note, used for tuning musical instruments.

Vowels: The letters *a*, *e*, *i*, *o*, and *u*. Their articulation is made by the absence of any obstruction in the vocal cords. The breath moves through the passage freely.

Index